The Solo Travel Guide: Just do it

Dee Maldon

Bookline & Thinker

The Solo Travel Guide: Just Do It

Bookline & Thinker

Published by Bookline & Thinker Ltd
7 Regent Court
Chipping Norton
OX7 5PJ
Tel: 0845 116 1476
www.booklinethinker.com

A CIP catalogue for this book is available from the British
Library.

This book is a work of fiction. Names, characters, places
and incidents are either a product of the author's
imagination or are used fictitiously.
ISBN: 9780995623507

Cover design by Gee Mac.
Printed and bound by Lightning Source UK

Contents

So why do it?

Why not?

Many people want to travel but, when they raise the topic among family and friends, they don't hear enthusiasm. Instead, there are excuses like, "Oh, yes, I would love to go to Borneo, Brisbane, Bali, but…we need a new garden fence, a new car, I don't like foreign food, don't want vaccinations, hate flying…"

There is always an excuse. Some people say they want to travel but, let's face it, they will never get around to it. This book is for those of you who want to get around to it, and who want to do it now. My question is why should you wait for others to join you when you could do it alone?

All you have to do is get out there – make the move to visit a new country, meet new people, see amazing sites, view another way of life. Do not let your friends' lack of enthusiasm or your fear of going alone hold you back. It is time to decide, "Would I rather make this trip, set off and explore, or stay at home and talk about it."

To me, the answer is easy – life is short, this day isn't coming back.

But setting out on a solo trip is not for the fearful. Recognise in advance that it is going to be lonely, you might get lost, something could go wrong and figure out how you might overcome these problems. Also be aware that you may face every single one of these occurrences just by staying home. I've taken train journeys near my home that have been laced with suspicious co-travellers, I've had missed connections and bad food and no one to commiserate with, share complaints or even laugh with – all in my own home territory.

Know that you can overcome these problems. If you feel lonely, watch people, call a friend for a chat or distract yourself by reading a book. If you get lost, ask directions, go to a café where you can discretely pull out a map. Something goes wrong, quickly figure out what is the worst thing that can happen and figure out how you will tackle it. I once lost my backpack – it was on a bus, the driver announced a ten minute break and I was in a queue buying coffee when he drove off – early! I quickly figured out that it wasn't the worst case scenario, I had my purse and my passport on me. But I didn't tell the bus inspector that. I lied and told him that my passport was in my backpack on the bus (wrong, I know, but I knew it would make them act and take care of my backpack). The inspector radioed to the next bus station and someone was there to rescue my backpack and keep it in a locked office until I could arrive there on the next bus.

However let's start by being honest, solo travel can be lonely, especially when watching a group of people at dinner, laughing together, or a couple of women at a girly lunch. My advice, watch them, enjoy their laughter, and later you will value those times with your own friends. And you can always pick up your mobile phone – a few buttons pressed and you can be chatting away to those who know you, laughing at your adventures, speculating on what will happen to you tomorrow. The conversation is likely to end with your friends wishing they were with you, and you feeling more than a little proud of your achievement.

Travelling solo will make you more independent. I no longer feel self-conscious about eating alone, although many people do and they take a book or journal to read over their meal. There is absolutely nothing wrong with doing this. Reading is a perfect distraction. However, through the years, I've learned to be quite brazen and I sit upright at my little table, enjoy wine with my meal, and watch those around me as though they were a show put on for my entertainment. I wonder about their stories, their backgrounds, relationships – and use my imagination to fill in the gaps. If the surroundings are not so interesting, then I pretend a companion has left briefly to visit the bathroom – I eat alone and carry on.

So, my advice is that no one should deny themselves the chance to travel because they fear doing it alone. Whether it is because your husband doesn't want to travel, your friends can't afford it or haven't made it a priority; you should not sit at home saying, "I wish I could go to…"

If you need inspiration on travelling alone, try reading *Daisy, Daisy* by Christian Miller. She was a grandmother when she set off on her first solo trip. She says that for her entire adult life she had always needed to tell her family where she was and how she could be reached – whether it was her mother, her children, her husband. But when she reached a time in life when her parents were dead, her children wrapped up in the lives of their own children, and her husband fully occupied, she knew that this was time for her own trip and she cycled alone across America.

Dervla Murphy started out by cycling from London to India and has covered much of Asia and Africa in her almost fifty years of travel. She is honest and sometimes brutal in her travelogues – something I relish. She gives startling advice on where to hide bank notes when travelling through dangerous places. Robbers, she says, always want to check inside your shoes and socks. In really risky areas she suggests putting the cash inside your vagina – and duly this paid off when she travelled through Russia and was robbed, even of the money she'd hidden in her socks and shoes. Dervla says she never tells her family her route or where they should expect her to be at any given time. They can't help her if she gets into trouble, she says, so she keeps to her own pace and her own rambling route. I love reading her journeys, a truly inspiring woman.

But even more inspiring perhaps are the women who took off across continents in previous centuries – without a guide book, a map and often with very little advice. These women ventured out with enthusiasm to see what was out there and, I have to confess, they are my role models. When I feel life is turning a little dull and a general discontent stirs within me, I reach for their stories and soon I am planning a trip far away, often a solo one.

You can read more of these inspiring women later in this book.

Before you go:

Travel planning

Where and when

For your first trip alone, you may want to try a weekend city break to somewhere that has always appealed to you. A weekend is not a long time alone, and a city provides the opportunity for the lone traveller to blend in. It will also provide a sense of how it feels to be alone in a strange place with only you to entertain and occupy. If a city break has no appeal, try somewhere that does appeal, but a weekend break is the perfect length for your first trip. Think hard about where you would like to go and imagine yourself there and try to envision how you will pass your time. This way you can research the activities available and plan in advance what you will see and do. By being busy you can avoid feeling alone for a whole weekend.

If it isn't a city you are visiting, then think about a small resort – somewhere without an overwhelming number of tourists but a place that is used to receiving visitors – large groups and small.

Smaller resorts have more time for the traveller, and you are treated as a person rather than a small part of the horde.

However, if you want to blend in then a large bustling beach town might provide the perfect camouflage. Others among you might prefer a lonely village, somewhere unused to travellers, a place where you can be alone.

We have a rundown of attractive places for the solo traveller towards the end of this book. However, your first venture should perhaps be closer to home. The idea is to try it for a weekend; this is a relatively short time to grow used to your own company in a strange locale.

Once you have made the decision, research the town or country you are visiting, know something about its politics, a brief history, the key places to visit, its social customs, and know of any dangers or civil strife that might flare up.

It's probably best to plan a solo visit during the shoulder season – between the peak and low period. The height of tourist season means crowds, the lone traveller can blend in at this time but it is hard to find places to sit in cafes, accommodation is expensive and tickets for events harder to come by. The low season often has 'closed' signs at main sites and the lack of other tourists means that the lone traveller stands out. Personally, I like to travel prior to peak season – it's the early part of the season, tourist staff at hotels, sites, transport often feel energised and are eager to greet visitors. In fact, they are happy to see you and often very hospitable.

Tips

Research, research, research

No matter where you are going, research the location – whether it is in your home country or abroad. Buy a good guidebook and learn the specifics of where you are visiting. A good book will help you grow familiar with the location in advance – sometimes it might turn you off a visit; but usually it makes you even more keen to go. If the book is light, take it with you. If it is hefty and you are taking an e-reader or tablet on the trip then buy the ebook. Otherwise, simply tear out the pages you need, and take them in a plastic sleeve. There is no need for any of us to carry heavy books.

Know opening hours, public holidays

There is no point in planning a trip and arriving to find shops, museums and major tourist sites are closed. Find out in advance what the regular rest days are and whether your trip coincides with any public holidays.

Travel insurance

A necessity, whether you keep it to simply health coverage in case of accidents or illness or whether you choose to add possessions and transport coverage. Know exactly how much you are covered for, what you need to do to make a claim (i.e. do you need to bring a police report from your trip?) how much is not covered in each claim (deductible) and report to the insurance company before your trip telling them all your health issues, medicines and tests. Hiding information will mean you forfeit health coverage if you make a claim.

Visas

Check whether you need a visa to enter the country you want to visit, you might be surprised at how many places require you to apply in advance to visit their country.

Money

Check your bank cards to ensure they do not expire while you are travelling. In addition, let the bank know which countries you are visiting and the dates. Also, through your bank, apply for some of the country's currency. Foreign exchange is expensive at airports, do this in advance. You may want to have some money aside in travellers' cheques.

Accommodation

Choose accommodation in a safe area. Before making a booking, read the guide books on the local areas. Also spend time on the hotel review sites where other travellers give advice on where to stay, what they liked and disliked about specific hotels. Also check Google maps and Google street view. These can be a terrific help in letting you know how close you are to main sites and whether an area looks downbeat and unsafe. Some travellers feel this takes away the romance of arriving and exploring a new area. However, if you're new to solo travel, then safety creates comfort – use Google and its street view for all they are worth.

As a general rule, it is best to avoid hotels and hostels near train stations. These areas are often associated with drug use and ladies of the night. A German friend once helped me choose a hotel in Frankfurt. Within hours of arriving she called and told me not to go out at night alone. "I just found out that this is a red light district," she said.

However, I was already out for dinner. Luckily, I had no problem until the morning when I was out walking and a man stopped me. I didn't understand what he was saying and pulled out a map to help him with directions. It was then I realised that this was not that kind of help he wanted.

Also avoid isolated accommodation that is fairly remote. This can make transport long, slow, not good at night and you may end up having to use taxis as a necessity.

Hostels are a good option for the solo traveller. Accommodation is cheap and often basic, you may be sharing a room with someone you've never met. But it is a good way to meet other travellers, hear their adventures and receive tips on places you plan to visit. Many travellers to hostels are solo, so you won't stand out – in fact, you'll be considered quite normal. However, don't leave valuables there. Most hostels offer lockers so take a padlock. Outdoor clothing shops often sell wire netting that fits over baggage. This can be padlocked in place for added security. I do not mean to scare you off hostels. I have never been robbed in one, but there are some things you simply need to be aware of.

Large hotels can feel anonymous and it's easy to feel alone and vulnerable in such places. I prefer smaller inns where the staff get to know you, recognise your face, remember your questions and have the time and knowledge to tell you about the area. Take care in hotels, never open the door to anyone – unless you have ordered room service of course. Even then, check through the peephole and keep the door on the chain until you have truly checked that they are bringing your meal.

When checking in, don't let the receptionist announce your room number out loud, they should simply talk moderately or pass the key to you with the room number on it. If they announce it in a loud voice ask for another room.

If you are a little nervous about staying alone in a strange place, take a rubber doorstop with you and wedge it under your door each night – no one will get in.

Medicines

Have enough of your prescription with you in your hand luggage. Keep the medicine in the normal packaging – otherwise it might be interpreted as illegal drugs. Carry a spare prescription or a letter from your doctor to say this is something you need.

Know the electrical currency

Whether it is to charge your phone or tablet or style your hair, you will probably need an electrical adapter.

Online guides will tell you which currency your destination uses, and you can buy an electrical adapter to plug your device into that will, in turn, be plugged into the wall. If you plan to travel a lot, purchase a multi-country adapter. They save money and anguish in the long run.

Communication

Look at your mobile tariff and consider taking out data roaming or add cover that includes your destination so that you can call home at any time.

Put your destination's emergency number for police and ambulance in your mobile – if there is an emergency then you won't have to look too far.

Laundry

Cut down on how much luggage you carry by bringing along a small container of detergent so that you can wash underwear, t-shirts, socks, etc. I use a small plastic bottle and decant detergent into this before travelling. Of course, put it in a sealed plastic bag in your luggage, you don't want any leaks.

What to take and wear

A wide topic this, especially for women, and it is, I believe, ruled by shoes. For instance, shoes you wear with jeans or trousers are often not suitable to wear with a skirt and vice versa. If you take both trousers and skirts then you are obliged to take several separate pairs of shoes or boots for each. However, if you choose to stick to trousers and jeans or dresses and skirts, your footwear is limited too.

Keep clothing simple. You're aim is not to dress to impress, but to get around without hassle or stares.

Comfortable walking shoes for sight-seeing are essential – whether you are in jeans or a dress. Try to avoid taking heels with you. They will hamper your movement, especially if out alone and can send the wrong message in some countries.

Take no expensive jewellery.

Finally, discern the clothes that will be acceptable at your destination. Cleavage and short skirts are fine for home, but they can offend when you are overseas. Know whether you need to keep your shoulders covered, whether skirts need to be below the knee, whether trousers might be frowned upon. Yes, it might seem like dictates from the dark ages to you, but you are in a foreign land and you wanted to travel, see new lands – well that's exactly what you're doing and they might do things differently there. Respect the local culture and its rules.

Plan your arrival

If you are flying to your destination, consider how you will travel from the airport to your accommodation. To me, arriving in a new country and stepping out of customs and immigration and into an airport arrivals hall is one of the most overwhelming experiences of any journey. You are in a new land and quite suddenly step through a door to be exposed to a gamut of signs pointing towards trains, buses, taxis, metro, often in differing languages, all while crowds of expectant hordes gaze at you, checking that you are not their long lost relative. At this point you are also vulnerable to drivers, legitimate taxi drivers and non-legitimate drivers, all keen to take your bags and drive you to wherever they think you want to go.

Most airports have a website giving information on connections to towns, local and not so local. These sites have links to train or bus schedules. They often give you other practical advice such as how much taxis cost to local towns. Plan your arrival so that you know exactly where you need to go and what mode of transport you need to get there. If you think you might need a take a taxi, refuse any offer of help as you step out of the arrivals hall and follow the directions to the airport's legitimate taxi stand.

Try not to arrive at your new destination after dark. This may mean you leave home before the cock has crowed or any cow has been milked, but it is worth it. Arriving late and finding your way around a new place after dark can feel a little threatening, especially if you're taking public transport. Daytime offers the ability to see your local streets, scout out a place for a decent meal, and look at the people around you. Night time drapes most streets in a threatening veil, and a late night arrival may mean no first day exploring or even an evening meal.

Luggage and bags

I do not believe the solo traveller is more vulnerable to thieves, but we do have to protect ourselves from any vulnerability. Therefore, I would recommend you choose cheap luggage and hand baggage. Thieves rate us on our bags, and my advice is to look like you have nothing to lose. No branded LVMH, Gucci – not even fake stuff as thieves don't know the difference from a distance. Buy a cheap handbag or bag before you leave home. I have a friend who walks through city streets with her things in a plastic supermarket bag – she's clearly sending out the message that she has nothing worth stealing.

Carry passport, credit cards, all valuables in a body wallet that is worn under your shirt – these can be found in most travel, hiking or book shops. Never dig this out in the street – go into a bathroom.

Keep coins and small denominations of money in your pocket. No mobiles or wallets in your back pockets, these are easy places for thieves to access – you might think you would feel someone pry in your nether regions, trust me, these people are good at what they do, you won't.

While you're there

Watch the locals to see how they do things. Watch how they greet each other, whether women and men react to each other differently, whether they bow, make eye contact or not. Look at how they're dressed. If the women don't wear shorts in the street, then you probably shouldn't. If they avoid eye contact with men, then you should too. You can learn so much by example and by following their lead, you will blend in.

Smile

A smile can get you a long way. And I don't mean a dippy smile that makes you look like you're on happy pills or the desperate smile we give to those who might rescue us from our own company. I mean a strong smile – the one that says you are in charge and confident. The one you use when you see a good friend who hasn't passed your door for a long time. This is the one you use when you enter a restaurant alone for the first time and you refuse to look down apologetically because it is only you seeking a table. This is the smile you use when you are genuinely happy to see someone. If it helps, use the old fashioned African greeting: "Hello, and how are you?" It carries warmth, shows confidence and that you are in charge and draws a response – for who can avoid replying that they are well and asking, "And how are you?"

Be open

As you visit new hotels or hostels, you will find other solo travellers who may be open to friendship, trips or dinners. Don't take it personally if another solo traveller is cold. They may genuinely want to be alone – for whatever reason. Also culturally, we are all quite different. My upbringing means I am culturally bound to be friendly, no matter my mood – it's as though my role in life is to reach out and offer the hand of friendship. It's not always taken. Sometimes others are wary of my effusive welcome – that may be part of their culture. Sometimes I worry that they look at me with suspicion – why is she being so friendly, what is she after? No matter, I like to think I'm perceived as welcoming and assertive.

It's also a good idea to be wary of putting out invites too quickly, or at least not until you've had more than a casual conversation. Some people travel alone because they genuinely do not like others or they like people who are similar to themselves.

I once shared a hotel terrace with a neighbouring room, and the woman there seemed to be fairly friendly – she didn't run away when I asked if she'd like a cup of coffee. It was a nice conversation – that was until she started to put down the locals and tell me how stupid and difficult they were. I had been about to ask her to dinner and was happy she'd shared her awful point of view before we shared wine and a hearty meal.

Travelling alone in Greece brings weary comparisons to Shirley Valentine. What can I say? Don't let the stereotype get you down. There are many women travelling Greece alone and why not? It's a beautiful country, good food, friendly people, need I go on? Most of us can tell an old Greek Romeo a mile off and it's up to each of us how we deal with him. A few cold words or a frozen shoulder see most of them off. However, if the idea of a brief romance takes you, have away.

Be cool, don't give too much of yourself away.

This may contradict the previous advice to be open. Communication is a two way street and, when you've been alone for a few days it is easy to pour out your entire history to someone you have only just met. Restrain yourself, for many reasons: You may decide later that you don't like or trust that person.

Be careful you don't give away too much information about yourself, information that makes them more familiar than you later decide is healthy.

Ask questions of other travellers

The best way to get to know someone, and judge whether you want to make them a friend is to ask questions – where are they from? Is an obvious one. But, "Why are you here?" "Have you been here before?" Questions on family, occupation, where else have they visited? Have they visited your home country? What is their home country like to visit?

People generally love to talk about themselves and will often get lost in the joy of sharing their history. It is amazing how quickly you get to know someone and learn whether you want to spend more time with them. There are few people in the world who are truly boring and asking questions is a fast and amazing way to make friends, learn more about the world and fine tune your art of conversation

Public places

Cafes, beaches, museums, etc are your best friend when travelling alone. As long as you are out in public it is rare that something bad can happen. For this reason, never go to a new friend's hotel room, home or even their car. If someone pressures you to take their hospitality, beware and back away from them quickly and in public. Never feel rushed to make a decision – whether it is to join someone on a trip or simply go for a drink with them. Back out. Pay attention to your instincts. If you're uncomfortable, retreat to a safe space.

It is a good idea to use the name of a fictitious friend who is meeting you – use this imaginary friend to your advantage and say you are meeting them later. It also tells the other person that you are not as alone as they might think you are and not as vulnerable. If an imaginary friend is a step too far for you, simply say that you have plans. You are under no obligation to tell anyone anything – "I have plans," is a shut case for any conversation, especially if you volunteer no further information.

I have shaken off persistent strangers (mainly men) with fake phone numbers or by saying I needed to go to the bathroom, buy a ticket at a train station, run to the supermarket or make a phone call – this is the best one – it lets the person know you're not alone in the world. You can get away – just be sure of your exit – taxi, train, bus, hotel, simply know exactly where you are escaping to and that the way is clear.

Out and about

Carry the name of your hotel and its address with you, just in case you become lost, disorientated or your transport links fail. If the country you are visiting uses a different alphabet or language then have the hotel name and address written in that language and script – this way it can be easily read by a taxi driver in Russian Cyrillic or Chinese characters.

When it comes to taxis, ask the hotel staff about how to recognise an official taxi – many cities have them in a specific colour – New York, yellow; London, black; Athens, yellow; Dubai, silver, etc. Stick to official taxi services, they may be more expensive but, generally, they are more trustworthy and safe. Taxis should be metered. Look for a meter when you get in, and tell the driver to turn it on. If he says it isn't working, or it's cheaper without the meter, get out and look for another taxi.

It's best to sit in the backseat of the taxi, sitting in the front is too familiar and may send the wrong message.

In some countries, India for instance, it is easy to negotiate a half day or full day rate with a taxi driver, simply tell him the place you wish to visit. Indian taxi drivers will take you to multiple destinations and give you the rate for a full or a half day. Another real benefit of this system is that this taxi driver will find you, no matter how busy the locale. So when you step out and see a sea of black cabs and wonder, "What the…How will?" He will find you, often sidling up closer so that you simply have to hop in. If he's been a good taxi driver, give him a healthy tip – this can make the difference in school fees for his child

If you feel the need to check a map or guide book, go into a café. Never check a map out in the street. Nothing signposts *tourist* quite like the map consultation.

Don't gawp. Look, admire, even take photographs, but do remember to try and blend in. You don't have to dress like a local, but if they don't wear shorts in a city street then neither should you. Skirts and dresses (for women) are a fairly universal way of blending in.

Walk with confidence, don't cower as though you're afraid of everyone who looks at you. If you feel a little threatened make eye contact with the person, let them know you've seen them, that you'll remember them and that you are not intimidated.

Don't wear a music headset, you need to be aware of what is going on around you, also listening to your music takes you out of your foreign setting.

Never forget the joy of people watching. So many people have their eyes on their mobile phones – reading, emailing, playing games – no one watches people these days. I love sitting near tourist sites and watching the travel world at leisure, guessing where people are from, who they're with, why they're here, and checking out their clothes. This is one of the world's greatest past times in my opinion.

In cafes, always have your bag on your lap or hooked over your knee. Never drape it across the back of your chair as it is too easily stolen.

Use your hotel, hostel, B&B host for information, ask about places to avoid, times to avoid, as well as where to go to.

Food and drinks

Don't take too much alcohol. Be aware of how you feel when you are drinking, don't go for just one more the way you might when you are with friends at home. Alcohol makes you vulnerable and likely to do things you might not do normally. In addition you are more susceptible to pressure from strangers, to abduction, violence – I don't think I need go on. Plus any accident you have while under the influence is likely to not be covered by insurance.

Common scams

These can happen to couples and groups, not just singles:

Street hawkers

Don't let anyone drape a scarf over your shoulder or give you a bracelet, heather, lavender, anything. Simply hand the object back or place it on their shoulder and keep walking.

Even if someone holds out a diamond ring and says you dropped it, do not take it. You will be asked for money for a worthless trinket.

Photographs

If you want a photo that isn't a selfie taken at 18 inches ask a fellow tourist. The tourist might even ask you to do the same for them. There are too many stories of locals demanding a fee or even running off with your camera or phone.

Fake police

If you are stopped by someone in uniform and asked for your passport, do not hand over any of your documents. If someone says they're police, tell them your passport is in the hotel safe. Don't offer to accompany them anywhere. Stay in the public spot and call or look for regular police. It is often a good idea to know the police emergency number in any new country you visit – even add it to your mobile before you go. If the people in uniform try to tell you that you've done something wrong and ask for a bribe – ask for identification and tell them you will call the police for verification. Don't go anywhere with these people, stay on the public street and pay nothing.

An accidental distraction – or is it?

If you feel something hit your shoulder or back and a kind stranger tells you it is bird poo, sauce or any number of substances, don't accept their help. Walk away. This is a fairly common way to have your wallet, purse, phone, etc stolen.

It is a good idea to leave your back pockets empty. Keep your valuables in a traveller's pouch inside your clothes. Crowded public spaces are a pickpockets dream. Do not make life easy for them. Only keep small change for snacks, bus fares, etc in your pockets.

If someone asks you to sign a petition, ignore them and walk on. While they are telling you about their cause, their friends will be deftly picking your pocket or handbag – or even cutting through your backpack.

Again, if someone stops you and asks if you speak English and that they want to visit there, ignore them. Do not worry about being bad mannered, because while you are engaged in conversation your belongings or pockets will be rifled through by someone else and your property stolen.

A more extreme example of this is when someone shoves a baby into your arms, leaving you too afraid to let go. You are left vulnerable while pickpockets go through your jacket, trouser and bags. At this point, shout out for help.

Money changing scams

Never take up any offer to change money on the black market, no matter the rate. Stick to banks and ATMs. It is not only illegal, but you may be trading good currency for counterfeit.

A chance to buy something precious

Whether it is gems, carpets, gold, currency, losing money on fakes is never a good deal. Be wary of that great deal you are offered by a friendly man or woman in a café/restaurant/shop. You often get far less than you paid for.

Overly helpful stranger

Be wary of the overly helpful guy at a train station who assists you in how to use the ticket machine, find the platform, locate your seat on a train or navigate a metro. He, it is usually a he, will want a tip.

ATM skimmers

Take no help from anyone when using an ATM – even if they tell you that you will have extra charges at that bank and they can show you another bank that charges nothing. Do not believe them. Don't let anyone near you when taking out money, stand with your body blocked against the machine if you have to. Don't let anyone other than a retailer, hotelier, etc even handle your card – card skimming machines are now small enough to fit in a pocket.

Ensure a retailer is not on the telephone while they are putting through your transaction – they could be taking a photo of your card.

Hide any pin numbers with an indiscrete hand when entering any code.

Fake wifi zones

Free wifi zones are often hacked. Those in the know set up in public spots knowing that victims are likely to be happy to connect. You can give away so much detail and your email passwords changed so quickly that you no longer have access to your mail. This can affect all your online accounts, including banking. Ask the hotel, hostel, café for the password to their wi-fi. It is not worth losing passwords and personal info to hackers.

Broken taxi meter

Sometimes the cab driver will tell you his meter is broken but he will give you a good rate. If you really want to go and you want to do it immediately, then negotiate a good rate ahead of time. If not, get out of the taxi and take one that does have a meter that works.

Your taxi driver tells your hotel is closed

Don't believe him. They want to take you to another hotel where they get a commission. Ignore his advice and tell him you called the hotel that morning and all is well (it's a lie but he doesn't deserve your goodwill). If you are staying in a hotel, it might be useful to call the hotel in advance and ask if they have an airport shuttle bus. If they don't, ask them for the contact details of a reputable taxi company to pick you up at the airport.

A helpful stranger tells you the attraction you wish to visit is closed

They'll try and guide you elsewhere, to a place they say is better. Ask around, don't be afraid. If the other diners in the café, or the people in a shop say the place is open then I would believe them. This is where your guide book comes in handy – check closure days for religious or public holidays.

Fake bus or train tickets

A helpful stranger offers to sell you travel tickets at a discount – usually they have a friend who is a travel agent. Often the tickets are not valid, they're fake, and you have lost your money. Always buy tickets at official offices.

Seductive flirt

Be wary of seduction. Men seem to fall for this more than women, possibly because women are more sceptical when a strange young man brings flattery to the table. It often happens in a café or bar, a young, attractive person of the opposite sex begins a conversation, creates a connection, and suggests going somewhere else. Either the evening ends up with a huge bill for cheap drinks or you end up drugged and wake up with no purse or wallet and needing the hotel to pay the taxi from the bar or wherever you wake up.

Beggars pull your heart strings

Beggars are hard to turn away from, especially when they are old, disabled or children. Be aware that they are often used by gangs precisely because they pull on our heart strings. Do not give money to beggars – you may be feeding an industry and often times thieves watch to see where you keep your cash and you may be robbed later. If you feel you must help, ask around about locally-run charities and give donations directly.

Someone needs help

Be wary of a stressed stranger trying to take you somewhere to help their wife, child, friend. This could be a scam and you are being led down a dark and lonely alley. Tell them you will call for help, but go nowhere with anyone.

In this vein, while driving, don't stop if someone tries to wave you down. Keep driving and call the police to help them when you are in a safe place.

Other tips

Leave diamond rings, expensive handbags, gold jewellery at home. Wearing these is like a sign to robbers saying you are open for business.

In your hostel or hotel:

Never open your door to strangers. If there is a knock on the door, use the peep hole or call through the closed door to ask who they are. Then call down to reception to confirm that they have sent someone. If you are still not happy that they are the cleaner, mini-bar checker, room inspector, whatever, simply don't open the door.

If someone calls the room phone, says they are reception and that their computer system has failed and they must have your credit card details immediately, hang up, it's a scam.

Fake fast food flyers might be put under your hotel room door. If you call, make an order and give your credit card details, do not be surprised if the food never appears. Also don't be surprised to find out that your card has been reproduced complete with cvc code (numerical code on the back that is used for purchases when the card holder is not there in person).

The best advice is that if it doesn't feel right, walk away. If it's too good to be true, then it often is. Pay attention to your instincts.

Health

Pay attention to how you feel.

If jet-lagged, try not to nap in the afternoon as this will mean you will not sleep in the evening. Have a relaxing day, take it slow and easy, don't do too much and you will sleep fine at the end of the day.

Drink plenty of water – bottled if necessary. Dehydration is common after long flights and especially if the climate is hot and you have been active. High altitudes, especially those over 2000 metres, also dehydrate the body, so be aware and stick to drinking water. If you are feeling light headed or faint, drink even more. The best way to check if you are dehydrated is to look at the colour of your urine – pale is best; dark amber means you need more fluids.

If you are very hot, don't step straight into arctic air-conditioning as this can make you feel quite ill. Try and sit in the shade for a short time before going into a chilled zone.

If you are in a mosquito zone then use mosquito repellent and mosquito nets around bedding. Malaria is not a friendly disease. Early signs of the disease are headache, chills and a fever – know these and get help immediately if you feel all three at the same time.

Take care with insect bites and don't scratch them. Remember that bites can become infected.

A suntan looks good but sunburn hurts and can be dangerous. We can burn even on cloudy days – in fact it is more likely to happen on a cloudy day because we often go out without sun protection on these days.

Remember that altitude affects sun burn – the higher we are, the more likely we burn.

Check whether the tap water is okay to drink. If the hostelry say it isn't then don't even brush your teeth with it – use bottled water always.

In addition, avoid food that is likely to have been washed in tap water such as lettuce, tomatoes, unpeeled fruit. It goes without saying that ice is made of water, if you can't drink the water, don't use the ice.

Fruit that has to be peeled by you is best. Bananas are wonderful as they have thick peels, provide good minerals and give energy – a perfect travel food (if only they didn't turn black quite so quickly).

Be wary of strange food, something your digestive system isn't used to can make you feel ill even though it isn't food poisoning.

Avoid foods that were cooked a while ago – the foods sitting on a counter for instance. Stick to hot foods that are prepared and cooked in front of you. Sizzling street food is, surprisingly, best.

Inspiration

Other guide books for the solo traveller often include essays from people who've gone alone, done it and have written about it.

I'm going to reach a bit further back than that. I'm going to tell you about the truly inspirational women travellers, those who went without a mobile phone, guide book or even a map. Many ordinary women from previous centuries defied everything that was expected of them when they set out to see the world. Married women were supposed to oversee their households, spinsters were expected to care for elderly relatives. Many of us know about the wealthy, titled ladies, such as Gertrude Bell, Lady Mary Montagu, Hester Stanhope, who have all been lauded as heroines, their exploits written about, praised and emulated. I prefer to highlight the women who had no access to lofty connections with grand homes in foreign lands, those women who simply stepped out of their family homes and launched themselves into truly extraordinary adventures.

These women set off because they wanted to see what was over a border or across a sea. They had an urge to experience new lands and make friends outside their own home.

The following are a few of my favourite women travellers.

Helen Caddick, 1842-1926

Helen Caddick was a single woman of means, a respected pillar of Birmingham society. She travelled because she loved the adventure. While visiting friends in southern Africa, she decided to take a trip to the interior. Everyone around her tried to persuade her not to go, saying it was dangerous. But she took a steamboat to what is now Malawi, and from there she hired 16 men to carry her and her luggage – 2 to carry her luggage and 14 to share the burden of carrying her in a hammock. She knew she would need a translator and took on a young boy from a local mission station whose English was entirely Biblical. He would respond to her summons with, "Behold, I am come."

Unlike male explorers who wrote to show their heroic exploits, women tended towards descriptions of events that were insightful and without prejudice. Helen Caddick is one such explorer.

"When I started on again a crowd of at least 50 women and children escorted me for quite a long distance, running by the side of the machila (hammock) laughing and talking all the time. I learnt

a curious thing here, namely, that if you beckon a native in the way we do, he will run away. The native way of beckoning is to point your finger towards the earth and to pull them towards you. In counting, the native puts his finger to his lips for one, and again for two. He holds up three fingers for three, and for four, two fingers of each hand. Five is the hand closed with the thumb poking out between the second and third fingers, and ten is the two closed fists on top of each other."

Of her camping cook, she is nothing but tolerant.

"On the second day, I boldly ventured into the improvised kitchen, but I soon came away somewhat horrified at the state of things I found there. The cook held a plucked fowl in one hand and was beating it with the other — black, I feared in both senses — to make it tender. As I wished to be able to eat my dinner, I never went on a tour of inspection again. As far as possible throughout the journey, I ate everything with my fingers, being doubtful of the knives, as I once saw the washing-up boy cleaning them in the way an unsophisticated schoolchild will clean his slate. I do not suppose for a moment my cook was worse than many of the native cooks, but I do not think visits to the kitchen are a wise proceeding on the part of those who want to enjoy their meals."

And it wasn't just the kitchen:

"At Kawimbe, the rats in the house were terrible at night. They raced about my room and scampered over my bed in a thoroughly happy manner. I could not sleep at first, but at last I got used to them, and dropped off only to wake up and find a rat with his foot in my ear."

She loved trading with the locals.

"I always enjoy the fun of bartering; it is so much more amusing than giving a fixed price in money. At Ikomba I bought a splendid stool belonging to a chief. It was chopped out of a solid piece of wood, and was beautifully polished by use. The owner was sitting on it, and the first to be done was persuade him to rise. Then I picked up the stool and offered him calico; at which he shook his head, and took hold of a leg of the stool. I held onto the other, and made my boy unroll more calico, till at last, he gave in. The chief greatly enjoyed the joke, as, of course, I gave him a great deal more than the stool was worth; but I wanted it as it was quite the best one I had seen."

A White Woman in Central Africa, Helen Caddick, 1900.

Ida Pfeiffer, 1797-1858

Ida was born in Vienna, an only daughter among five brothers. She married a much older man, chosen by her father, and lived a traditional life, raising two sons. At the age of 45, she was widowed with sons who were grown and independent. She had always wanted to travel and believed she should start with a visit to the Holy Land. Friends tried to dissuade her, called it a dangerous pilgrimage, and preposterous for a woman alone. However, she writes, *"I made my will, and arranged all my worldly affairs in such a manner that, in case of my death (an event I considered more probable than my safe return), my family should find everything perfectly arranged."*

Ida was robbed and cheated but came back nine months later exhilarated and keen to see more of the world. She sold her belongings and began writing travel journals to fund future journeys. Her adventures became so popular that she was often offered free passage on ships and trains in the hope of a mention. Her books were translated into many languages. She was the first female travel diarist – a beacon for the rest of us to follow.

Her description of crossing the Nile to climb the Egyptian pyramids, *"Two large powerful men stood side by side; I mounted on their shoulders, and held fast by their heads, while they supported my feet in an horizontal position above the waters, which at some places reached almost to their armpits, so that I feared every moment that I should sit in the water. Besides this, my supporters continually swayed to and fro because they could only withstand the force of the current by a great exertion of strength and I was apprehensive of falling off. This disagreeable passage lasted above a quarter of an hour."*

Her advice for taking a sea voyage:

"Passengers would do well to take with them a few additions to the ship's fare. The suitable are: portable soup and captain's biscuit – both of which should be kept in tin canisters to preserve them from mouldiness and insects – a good quantity of eggs, which, when the vessel is bound for a southern climate, should be first dipped in strong lime-water or packed in coal-dust; rice, potatoes, sugar, butter...I would recommend those who have children with them to take a goat as well."

On visiting Canton, China: *"On my way from the vessel to the factory, both old and young turned back to look after me, and that they hooted and pointed at me with their fingers; the people ran out of the booths and gradually formed a crowd at my heels. I had, however, no alternative but to preserve my countenance; I walked, therefore, calmly on, and perhaps it is to this very fact of my manifesting no fear that I escaped unmolested."*

On her last journey, this was to Madagascar:

"Our vessel was an old worn-out brig of war, which in her youthful days formed part of the British fleet at the great victory of Trafalgar in 1805. Deeply had she fallen from her former high estate; for now, in her old age, she was used for carrying oxen during the fine season of the year from Madagascar to the Mauritius. Accommodation for passengers was

none, all the space being divided into berths for the oxen; and as to the security of our vessel, the captain gave me the consolatory assurance that she was utterly unfit to do battle with anything approaching to a storm." My desire to leave Mauritius behind me was nevertheless so great that nothing could dissuade me from going. I commended myself to Heaven, embarked with a light heart, and had no reason to repent my boldness. If the ship was bad, her captain, Mr. Benier, was a remarkably good one. Though not of high birth, for he was half Creole in colour, he behaved with a courtesy and consideration which would have done honour to the most cultivated man. He at once gave up his cabin to me – the only place in the ship not monopolized by preparations for the four-footed passengers."

Ida Pfeiffer died at home in her native Vienna, aged 62.

A Visit to the Holy Land, 1852; *Travelling in China, A Lady's Journey Around the World*, 1851; *A Visit to Madagascar*, 1861.

Mary Hall, 1857-1912

Like Helen Caddick before her, Mary Hall loved setting out with only local bearers, guides and cooks as companions. However, Miss Hall came not from a gentrified background with money as a safety net to fund her travels. Rather, she was the daughter of a gasfitter and was born in Southwark.

Her first trip was the length of Africa. She covered the 7000 miles with a series of Africans in her employment. Also, along for the journey, was her dog Mafeking who was to warn her of any danger from wild animals. Mary Hall had that doughty almost clichéd indomitable spirit of travelling women of the era. She would hang wet clothes from her hammock to dry and continue her march in a petticoat because she knew she would meet no one who believed it mattered.

Her reason for taking the journey was interesting:

"As I am the first woman of any nationality to have accomplished the entire journey of Cape to Cairo, I think perhaps a simple account of how I managed to do it quite alone may be of use to many who, for various reasons, real or imaginary, are unable to go so far afield. I hope that a book, written from a woman's point of view, minus big game romances, and the usual exaggerations incidental to all things African, may be acceptable."

She knew exactly who she was and why she was doing the journey.

Later, Mary Hall wrote a second travel book detailing her adventures in the Far East. She loved hearing about communication with Chinese servants, and a man she met explained how it worked:

"'Before time b'long collie' meant 'Formerly he was a coolie'; or that 'He savey have do before time

plenty'; was in plain English, 'He has done it many times already'. One day, Mr B told me he had been finding fault with his boy regarding extravagance in shopping, when the latter retorted, 'More better you catchee missee'; in other words, 'You had better get married.'"

Mary Hall's travel diaries sold well and she died in genteel Hampstead leaving an estate of over £7000 (when most estates were less than £1000).

A Woman's Trek from Cape to Cairo, 1907; *Travels in the Antipodes and in the Far East*, 1914.

Isabella Bird, 1831-1904

Isabella Bird was the daughter of an English minister. A back injury meant her parents encouraged activity and gave her free rein in horse riding and rowing. She took her first trip overseas to see relatives in the United States. Her father gave her £100 and told her to take her time. The trip was a safe one and gave her a hunger for travel to other foreign parts. However, for most of her early life, at least until she was 40, she lived at home taking care of her aging parents. Her first long trip was to Australia, not somewhere she seemed to like, and then on to Hawaii, where she later returned. Her real travel writing and adventures arose when she crossed the Rocky Mountains. She had arrived on the west coast of the United States and travelled alone on horseback through the Rockies. She is said to have had a romance with a wild outlaw she described thus: *"A knife in his belt, and a 'bosom friend', a revolver, sticking out of the breast pocket of his coat; his feet, which were bare, except for some dilapidated moccasins made of horse hide. The marvel was how his clothes hung together, and on him. The scarf around his waist must have had something to do with it. His face was remarkable. He is a man about forty-five, and must have been strikingly handsome. He has large grey-blue eyes, deeply set, with well-marked eyebrows, a handsome aquiline nose and a very handsome mouth. His face was smooth-shaven except for a dense moustache and imperial. Tawny hair, in thin uncared-for curls, fell from under his hunter's cap and over his collar. One eye was entirely gone, and the loss made one side of the face repulsive, while the other might have been modelled in marble. 'Desperado' was written in large letters all over him."*

Her writing dispelled any romantic sense of life for the settlers in the Rockies. She described their lives as so unhappy, they seemed cut off not just from civilisation but from any pleasure in their daily lives.

At home, a doctor friend chased her for marriage but she refused until her sister, who had ill health and who Mary cared for when she returned home, had died. She married John Bishop when she was 50, but when he died five years later she took off on her next adventures, this time to the Far East.

Of her arrival in Japan: *"As no English lady has yet travelled alone through the interior, my project excites a very friendly interest among my friends, and I receive much warning and dissuasion and a little encouragement. The strongest, because the most intelligent, dissuasion comes from Dr. Hepburn, who thinks that I ought not to undertake the journey, and that I shall never get through to the Tsugaru Strait. If I accepted much of the advice given to me, as to taking tinned meats and soups, claret, and a Japanese maid, I should need a train of at least six pack-horses. As to fleas, there is a lamentable consensus of opinion that they are the curse of Japanese travelling during the summer, and some people recommend me to sleep in a bag drawn tightly around the throat, others to sprinkle my bedding freely with insect powder, others to smear the skin all over with carbolic oil."*

A Lady's Life in the Rocky Mountains, 1897; *Unbeaten Tracks in Japan*, 1880.

Mary Eyre

Miss Eyre was a poor spinster taken with the idea that she could live more frugally on the continent than she could in Yorkshire. In her guide book she says she set out with, *"only one small waterproof stuff bag, which I could carry in my hand, containing a spare dress, a thin shawl, two pencils, paper, the inevitable 'Murray' (a guide book), and a prayer-book, so that I had no trouble or expense about luggage."*

Mary Eyre continued her journey to Spain, where she says, *"Near me, three young Englishmen were enjoying themselves with two pretty Spanish girls they had picked up in Malaga; they knew no Spanish, the senoritas no English, but this made them all the merrier. They were the first English tourists I had seen since I entered Spain; they grew a little intoxicated, and they were also the first drunks I had seen in Spain."*

A Lady's Walks in the South of France, 1865

Margaret Fontaine (1862-1940)

Margaret Fontaine loved butterflies and romance – in that order. She grew up in Norwich, daughter of a minister, but ran away to Ireland at age 21 in pursuit of a chorister. He apparently did not return her admiration, and she took herself off through Europe, falling in love with men along the way. She had learned about butterflies from a family friend and became an accomplished collector and illustrator, the culmination of her collection was eventually donated to Norwich Castle. However, it was while visiting Damascus that she fell in love with a married dragoman (guide and translator). He was 24, she was 39. They travelled the world together, collecting butterflies, both growing reputations as entomological experts. The relationship lasted until Khalil died 27 years later.

47

However, Margaret's eye for men remained. When being pursued by an admirer in west Africa, while she was well over the sixty she writes: *"I tried to reason with myself, recalling that my advanced years must stand as a barrier between all possibility of this passion being returned; but then no one thinks of me anything like as old as I am – even Lisle Curtois, barely two years ago had looked at me and said: 'Why, Margaret, to look at you, you might still be in your forties.' And Charles (Khalil), my own dear Charles, how often has he said: 'You have an attraction.' But I was a fool."*

Margaret, I salute you!
Love Among the Butterflies, 1986

Mary Kingsley (1862-1900)

Mary Kingsley is probably the best known of the Victorian women travellers (especially if we discount those titled ladies who travelled as distinguished guests staying at grand homes in foreign lands). Mary had little formal education but made good use of her father's library and was given access to academics and their conversations through family connections. On this, the young Mary thrived. However, she was a dutiful daughter, taking care of her aging parents until they died. At this point, aged 43, Mary wrote to English traders and missionaries in West Africa telling of her plans to visit and asking for advice and assistance. She is famous for arriving in complete Victorian garb – full skirts, high-necked blouses, fully-laced boots and said that British women in Africa should never dress in a manner they would not wish to be seen at home. She also credits her full skirt with saving her life when she was trekking with local guides: *"I made a short cut for it and the next news was I was in a heap, on a lot of spikes, some fifteen feet or so below ground level, at the bottom of a bag-shaped game pit. It is at these times you realise the blessing of a good thick skirt. Had I paid heed to the advice of many people in England, who ought to have known better, and did not do it themselves, and adopted masculine garments, I should have been spiked to the bone and done for."*

Mary caused controversy when she came home for criticising the missionaries and their arrogance with the Africans they sought to control. She died in South Africa of typhoid aged 48.

Travels in West Africa, 1897.

Others Victorian writers simply offered advice to those thinking about taking off in exploration:

"Wear a broad-brimmed hat to make parasols unnecessary. Small rings can be sewn into the hem of your skirt, a cord passed through the rings, it can all be pulled in quickly to keep it dry and so that it doesn't swish rocks downhill on hikes" Mrs H.W Cole, *A Lady's Tour round Monte Rosa; with Visits to the Italian Valleys*, 1859

Harriet Martineau (1802-1876) recommends that ladies not take a maid with them on their travels. *"No lady who values her peace on the journey, or desires any freedom of mind or movement, will take a maid."* She attributes this to the fact that maids turn easily to tears because of the hardships of travel.

These women have much in common – they defied the conventional life of parlour society and took off on adventures of their choosing. Of course, we know about their journeys because these adventuresses made it home and published accounts of their journeys. It is true that we know nothing of the women who didn't make it home – the same is true of the male explorers. We salute them all!

However you don't need to be an explorer sharing beds with cockroaches and rats while blazing into unchartered territory to be a solo traveller. You can simply make your own journey, enjoy the locale and return home satisfied with all you have experienced.

Suggested destinations

There are many places ideal for the novice solo traveller. We've pulled together a few suggestions, offering an overview of each locale. This is not a replacement for a good guide book, simply a small taster for those wondering where they should visit. And for those who like a good read, I've added a novel set in that location, something to give the place another dimension.

Europe

Barcelona

Barcelona is a modern city with an outdoor lifestyle. Markets, churches, architecture, restaurants, beaches, boulevards are perfect for any explorer who loves to be independent. The city is Spain's second largest (1.6 million in habitants). It was founded on ancient roots, Hannibal's father settled here in the 3rd century BC and, from there, it was a Roman settlement before being taken over by the Goths, North Africans, French and finally Spanish – although it still has a streak of independence and a strong movement toward Catalan home rule.

An airport bus, Aerobus, connects the airport with the city centre. The bus runs every 10—20 minutes and takes around 30 minutes.

The Metro system (stations are marked *M*) connects most of the city – from the beach to the Olympic hillside. For tourists who don't want to grapple with public transport, there is the Barcelona Bus Turistic made up of three bus lines – blue, red and green routes that explore different parts of the city. You can get on and off at any point. Normally, I stay away from these double-decker tourist explorers, but for a city as large as Barcelona, the system makes getting from beach to cathedrals to hillside parks very easy. There are also walking tours for those with very comfortable shoes.

Barcelona offers so much to visitors that I couldn't possibly tell you what to visit. But items not to miss are, in my opinion, the architecture of Antoni Gaudi which includes his unique cathedral, La Sagrada Familia which remains unfinished, his apartment building, La Pedrera which has no straight lines on its exterior, and his idealistic Parc Guell, a colourful complex on a high hillside.

Within the city of Barcelona you could spend a day or more walking Los Ramblas, a wide pedestrian tree-lined promenade that is a wonderful place to watch people, taste great food, wine and enjoy life. Nearby is the Placa de Catalunya, the main square with fountains, street artists and restaurants. The Gothic Quarter is walking distance with its network of squares that stretch back to Medieval and Roman times.

This city offers so much – a medieval city, art museums, flamenco dancing, cable car to the top of Montjuïc, need I go on? Tours to local vineyards are available as are boat trips that will show you the local coastline.

And let's not forget that Barcelona is a city with beautiful beaches – all relaxed, lined with cafes and restaurants. The beachfront boardwalk stretches for miles – a great place for exercise and sun. Some of the beaches are stoney, so be careful. Also, for the more straight laced among us, be aware that topless areas and clothing optional beaches are often unmarked.

Barcelona has a wonderful buzz that is infectious. This means that the lone traveller should never really feel alone.

Downside: Barcelona is the pickpocket capital of Europe. Carry nothing of value in your pockets or handbag. A body pouch is a certain necessity in this city.

To read: *Shadow of the Wind* by Carlos Ruis Zafon. Set at the end of World War II but a little Gothic in nature, this novel tells of a boy taken by his father to the Cemetery of Forgotten Books and given the opportunity to choose one title. As he moves into adulthood, he finds someone else, someone with dark designs, also seeks this book.

Munich

Munich is the capital of Bavaria. It was founded in the 11th century after a bridge was built across the River Isar, next to a Benedictine monastery, an important crossing place that soon saw the growth of a fortress. Munich's city centre sits now within these old fortifications. It offers rich shopping and plenty of good cafes, bakeries and restaurants. In addition, these old city walls encircle the Residenz, the former palace of Bavarian kings, which was once moated and has been expanded hugely over the last 700 years. Also in the city centre is the Glockenspiel, a wonderfully theatrical clock that enacts stories from the 16th century at set times during the day.

Slightly further afield, you will find Baroque palaces such as Nymphenberg and Schlossheim, with wonderful parks and art galleries. On a slightly darker note, Dachau Concentration Camp is around 10 miles from town. Trains go there from Munich's main train station every ten minutes and the journey takes less than 15 minutes.

Transport in Munich is well organised with a network of trains – S-Bahn is the suburban rail; U-Bahn is underground and there are trams and buses.

The S-Bahn connects Munich Airport with the city at frequent intervals depending on the time of day or night.

Munich is especially busy during Oktoberfest, a beer festival that began in the 19th century to celebrate a royal wedding, and also in the Christmas market season, which runs from late November to Christmas Eve. Expect wooden toys and ornaments, cakes and Gluwien. The hot mulled wine stands require a deposit for each mug. This means that locals stand chatting at the stalls while drinking. As a result, the solo traveller is never alone.

The downside of Munich is that it is a commercial city, one that works hard and sometimes has little patience for tourists. Natives of Munich also have a reputation for being a little snobbish and very brand conscious.

To read: *The Book Thief* by Markus Zusak. Narrated by death himself, this novel tells of a little girl sent to a foster family in 1939. She reads *The Grave Diggers Handbook* each evening with her foster father and, as her love of reading grows, she steals a book from a Nazi book burning. From this, her renegade life begins.

Stockholm

Sweden's capital is an expansive and peaceful place for solo travellers. It is made up of 14 islands, connected by 50 bridges all within Lake Mälaren which flows out into to the Baltic Sea. Several main districts encompass islands and are connected by Stockholm's bridges. Norrmalm is the main business area and includes the train station, hotels, theatres and shopping. Östermalm is more upmarket and has wide spaces that includes forest. Kungsholmen is a relaxed neighbourhood on an island on the west of the city. It has a good natural beach and is popular with bathers. In addition to the city of 14 islands, the Stockholm Archipelago is made up of 24,000 islands spread through with small towns, old forts and an occasional resort. Ekero, to the east of the city, is the only Swedish area to have two UNESCO World Heritage sites – the royal palace of Drottningholm, and the Viking village of Birka.

Stockholm probably grew from origins as a place of safety – with so many islands it allowed early people to isolate themselves from invaders. The earliest fort on any of the islands stretches back to the 13th century. Today the city has architecture dating from that time. In addition, it didn't suffer the bombing raids that beset other European cities, and much of the old architecture is untouched.

Getting around the city is relatively easy by metro and bus. There are also pay-as-you-go Stockholm City Bikes. The metro and buses travel out to most of the islands, but there are also hop on, hop off boat tours. It is well worth taking a trip through the broad and spacious archipelago, which stretches 80 kms out from the city.

Please note that taxis are expensive and, to make matters worse, the taxi industry has been deregulated leading to visitors unwittingly paying extortionate rates. A yellow sticker on the back window of each car will tell you the maximum price that the driver will charge therefore, if you have a choice of taxis, choose the one with the lower rate.

A few unique things to see in Stockholm include the Nobelmuseet, the Nobel Museum, which tells of the creation of the Nobel Prize and the creativity of its laureates, and the Spiritmuseet, where you can learn about the nation's complicated relationship with alcohol. Sweden is associated with design (and not just Ikea) and many shops sell Swedish-only design.

Oudoor activities in summer include hiking trails through the islands and archipelago. Winter activities stretch to cross-country skiing, ice skating and snow hiking.

Nightlife is expensive, cover charges to bars can be high and, bizarrely, the minimum age for drinking varies in an arbitrary fashion as it is up to each establishment to make its own decision – it can be anything from 17 to 27. So take identification with you.

There are two airports serving Stockholm. Arlanda is 40 kms north of the city and serves main airlines. Skavsta, 100 kms to the south, serves the budget airlines. Both airports have coaches to take visitors directly to the city centre.

Downside: Many independently owned restaurants and cafes close for holidays between July and August which can limit the range of places to eat.

To read: *The Girl with the Dragon Tattoo* by Stieg Larsson. This trilogy of a financial journalist and the tattooed genius with a motive to fight the dark right-wing forces of Swedish society romped through the bestseller lists.

Dubrovnik, Croatia

Dubrovnik's old architecture, all wrapped within its ancient stone walls, have made this city a World Heritage Site. It's an old sea port that sits above the Adriatic Sea. Its background, from medieval times was trade between the east and Europe and the city rivalled Venice for its reach and connections. Today, however, the principle economy is based on tourism.

The old town is a warren of narrow, cobbled streets, sometimes steep, but pedestrianised which makes it easy to walk. However, be careful – signs do not always point to where they say they are going – many of them are old and the hotels, restaurants, bus stations have moved. The City Walls might look familiar to fans of *Game of Thrones*

– many scenes were filmed here and there are *Game of Thrones* tours to visit the film's settings.

The area suffered a devastating earthquake in the 17th century, therefore much of the original architecture did not survive. The Sponza Palace, near the Bell Tower, is one of the few Gothic buildings left in the city. The Stradun is the main street in the Old Town – restaurants, shops and bars all pour out onto here. It's lively, especially towards the end of the day.

Don't forget that the city's location on the coast means that it also has beautiful beaches. Lapad Beach is two miles outside of town, and has a chilled atmosphere. Banje Beach is closer to the old town. It has an entrance fee and is livelier.

One of the reasons Dubrovnok appeals to solo travellers is because it has a low crime rate. In addition, its cobbled streets and artistic shops all make browsing easy.

Downside: I'm not sure there is one.

To read: I could find no good novels set in or around Dubrovnik, so I'm proposing you take *Rick Steve's Dubrovnik* by Rick Steves.

Norwegian fjords

As amazing as it might sound, you can travel the Norwegian coast, viewing astounding scenery, all on public transport – it simply takes planning.

By flying into Bergen – an airport bus will take you downtown – you can start a journey that will take you as far as the Arctic Circle. Trains, ferries and buses connect most Norwegian towns and villages. In fact, Norway has one of the best public transport systems in the world. It will take preparation, and it won't be cheap, although there are bus, train and ferry passes on offer to tourists – usually for packages of five days or ten.

Norwegians are polite and some may consider the natives to be a little cold, but they will never harass you or overwhelm you with questions. You will be able to dine alone without a curious stare in your direction.

Downside: The ferries can face some wild weather, stick to land transport if you are likely to suffer from seasickness.

To read: Norway is famous for its Nordic Noir brand of crime fiction. King here is Jo Nesbo but other great Norwegian crime writers are Anne Holt and Karin Fossum.

Edinburgh

For those who like walking, Edinburgh reigns supreme. The Royal Mile runs through the centre of the tourist area connecting Edinburgh Castle with Holyrood Palace. It's a little over a mile and, in addition to passing old Edinburgh historic sites, it is lined with independent shops, cafes and pubs along the way. For this is Edinburgh's Old Town, all cobbled streets beneath the lofty castle. The New Town is less than ten minutes walk away and it's far from new. Instead New Town is Georgian, built by the wealthy residents in the 18th century. Its wide streets and perfect proportions create a visual joy for walking. It's tough to name Edinburgh's main sites, but here goes: the castle, continuously occupied for more than 1000 years; Holyrood Palace, the Queen's official residence in Scotland; Mary King's Close, a preserved 18th century tenement on the Royal Mile and; the Grassmarket, a network of cobbled lanes with independent shops and cafes. I could go on.

Edinburgh is particularly busy during the festival that takes place from August to early September. It began as a military tattoo, developed into a fairly high brow arts festival and has expanded to host off-stage events from the clever to the bizarre.

Edinburgh also hosts a massive Hogmanay, or New Year, celebration with music and dancing in the streets all through the night and often into the next day. The city is at its busiest during the August festival and again at New Year.

Public transport by bus and tram is available from the airport to the city centre.

Downside: It is an expensive place to visit at peak periods and it can be tough to find a place to stay. Your first visit should be at quieter times.

To read: Edinburgh is a literary city and so many novels have been set here. *The Heart of Mid-Lothian* by Sir Walter Scott might satisfy those historians among you. For contemporary novels, you are spoiled for choice. The gritty *Trainspotting* by Irvine Welsh, *44 Scotland Street* by Andrew McColl Smith, *The Prime of Miss Jean Brodie* by Muriel Spark or one of my favourites *One Good Turn Deserves Another* by Kate Atkinson and featuring her ex-detective Jackson Brodie.

Venice, Italy

Venice is probably the most beautiful and unique city in existence. Everyone should visit it, at least once in their life. The grand houses, the canals, the varying light, it is a feast for the eyes. Venice is an ideal destination for the solo traveller because with so much to look at, who needs a companion? Who even needs to talk?

Venice sits in northern Italy, atop 120 islands within the shelter of a lagoon. She, because with such beauty she is certainly female, is the perfect city for walking and basking in Byzantine and Renaissance architecture.

The islands were initially inhabited in the early centuries by those seeking shelter from marauding Visigoths. With the decline of Rome, it was ruled as an early Christian city from Constantinople. As the that empire declined, Venice was in a good position to independently build on the old Byzantine trading links. And it did so, linking east and west with ideas, goods and politics.

Venice has its own airport, and water buses and coaches will take passengers into Venice itself. If you really want to arrive in style then there are water taxis to take you directly to your hotel. Getting around within Venice is easy as a network of Vaporetti, or water buses, ply the canals taking passengers from Saint Marks (San Marco) to the train station (Ferrovia) to Rialto (the iconic bridge across the Grand Canal) to the Lido, a long island with a terrific beach on the outer side of the lagoon. But Venice is best seen by walking and, despite the network of alleyways you truly cannot get lost. Signs are everywhere, pointing to *Rialto, San Marco, Ferrovia*, etc. You simply have to know where you want to go in relation to these popular destinations. There are also narrow boats, traghetto, that take passengers directly across the canals for two euros.

Saint Mark's Square is probably the best known tourist site, surrounded as it is by the Doge's Palace, which includes Casanova's jail; the Clock Tower with its astronomical workings; the Bell Tower and Saint Mark's Basilica.

But step down lanes, lose yourself, enjoy the everyday scenes of Venetian's at their life. Find the Jewish quarter, the markets near Rialto Bridge. And don't forget to visit the islands – Murano with its glass blowing and Burano, which is famous for lace.

Probably the best time to visit Venice is during Carnival, or Mardi Gras – the historic meat-eating period of great naughtiness before the time of Lent. Venice knows how to do this festival which harks back to high Christian times within the city when masks were worn so a person could behave badly without fear of recognition. Walking home at night, amid misty canals, and coming across Renaissance revellers is sometimes a little creepy, but the historic clothing takes the visitor back in time to the city's high point.

Downside: The cruise ships that ply the Grand Canal block out the sun and treat the beautiful city like it is a Disney attraction.

To read: *A Thousand Days in Venice* by Marlena de Blasi. The true story of an American food writer who receives a note from a Venetian stranger asking to meet for coffee. A grand romance takes place and de Blasi is good at pointing out the difficulties of life in Venice and the compromises we make in relationships, especially mature ones.

Salzburg, Austria

A compact town in central Austria, Salzburg is easy to get around by walking or by bike (available for rent). Mozart was born here in 1756 when the town was a prominent and rich principality. The wealth came from the nearby salt mines, hence the name, Salzburg, which means salt fortress. A hefty toll was placed on barges transporting salt on the River Salzach, and the town soon grew prosperous.

The Hohensalzburg Fortress sits above the town and offers terrific views of the nearby Alps. The fort offers a good tour, as does the Schloss Hellbrunn, a summer palace with gardens and fountains. Mozart's Geburtshaus, birth house, is a museum beautifully and timely decorated.

Modern culture associates Salzburg with *The Sound of Music* and there are now tours to the film's sites, complete with music.

A trolley bus brings passengers from the airport. The trip takes around 20 minutes.

Downside: The roads in Salzburg are narrow and the traffic can feel oppressive.

To read: *The Salzburg Connection* by Helen MacInnes, a popular spy fiction writer. Nazi secrets, sealed chests, Austrian Alps and all leading to a violent end.

Iceland

A self-contained island made up of lava fields, glaciers and rugged landscape with waterfalls, geysers and thermal seams that smoke, Iceland is one of the most unique places to visit. It sits close to the Arctic Circle and, as a result, has the long summer nights and very short winter days that can be quite disorientating to those used to more consistent sunrises and sunsets.

Reykjavik is the capital city, with a population of around 200,000. It was considered little more than a farm to the Danes but grew as a trading centre in the 18th century. It became independent of Denmark in 1918.

Reykjavik itself feels like a suburb of bright coloured homes. Getting around on foot is easy although you might want to take a tour bus to explore the outlying landscape.

The Golden Falls of Gullfloss, around 60 miles from the city, are an expansive set of double waterfalls. Six miles from the falls is a geyser that reliably spouts every ten minutes. However, these are just a few of the natural must-see sites in Iceland's landscape.

On the outskirts of Reykjavik is the Blue Lagoon, Iceland's most famous tourist site. The geothermal spa sits in a lava field, giving the water its 'blue' tinge. The spa is open to the public, but you do have to pre book.

For those who really love the outdoors, Iceland offers whale watching off its coast, while tours to the interior show a landscape that truly could be from another planet.

For the solo traveller, Iceland offers a unique package of language, people and landscape combined with a culture that values gender equality.

Downside: Iceland is expensive. Whether it is food, beer, wine, clothing, expect to pay far more than you would at home.

To read: The old classic *Journey to the Centre of the Earth* by Jules Verne begins at an Icelandic volcano. If you would like something more contemporary, you could try *Burial Rites* by Hannah Kent – the story of a woman sent to an isolated farm to await execution for murder.

North America

Seattle

Seattle is a modern American city surrounded by the most striking scenery of the Pacific-Northwest – it stretches from the waters of the Puget Sound to the Cascade and Olympic Mountain ranges.

It was founded on the fishing and logging industries. Later, Boeing aircraft made a home here and then the 1970s recession appeared destined to kill all industry in the city. But then Microsoft launched here, its garage origins are well known. The company grew and attracted other technological industries. The rest, as they say, is history. The city's career path had changed. Today, Seattle is a progressive community that takes a kinder and gentler approach to the issues that divide many US cities, such as social diversity and multiculturalism. It's a city that looks out to the ocean and, like most sea-facing regions, is outward in attitudes. Although the locals tend to be reserved but polite.

Another international company with its roots here is Starbucks, and their very first coffee shop still sits near Pike Place. American coffee culture is strong here, and the city has a relaxed atmosphere. The locals value good food and the surrounding area even offers own vine yards, so wine knowledge is strong.

The Light-Link-Rail connects the airport with the city centre and takes about 35 minutes.

The downtown area has much to occupy the visitor – from the Space Needle to Pike Place market with its famous fish salesmen whose wit draws in buyers as they toss their hefty trawl from seller to buyer.

The Monorail connects the downtown area with the Space Needle and the pier. From there you can take a ferry or water taxi and enjoy the view of Seattle and its mountains from a greater distance.

Downside: The weather can be wet – locals say they don't suntan, they rust! There can be extreme snow storms in winter and heatwaves in summer. So choose well when it comes to timing your visit.

To read: *Fifty Shades of Grey* by E.L. James was certainly set in this rainy city; as was *Where'd You Go, Bernadette* by Maria Semple. Both contemporary stories for this home of Microsoft and Starbucks.

Ashland, Oregon

Ashland in southern Oregon is a beautiful university town that sits at the foothills of the Siskiyou and Cascade mountains, about 20 miles north of the California Border. It's primary place on the tourist map comes from the Oregon Shakespeare Festival , the award-winning repertory theatre group that puts on eleven plays on three stages between the months of February to December.

It's a small town, walkable, with lots of good restaurants, cafes and art galleries. The locals are pretty tolerant and sometimes the place has an almost sixties hippy feel. Students from the local university, Southern Oregon University, make up a sizable chunk of the 20,000 population. Food here is often organic, especially the pears, peaches and apples which come from the surrounding orchards. Much of the wine is also local and comes from vineyards around the local Rogue Valley. Cafe service often comes with a heartfelt sense that we all need to pause and enjoy the environment.

Much of the downtown area has been preserved and is on the National Historic Register. Before settlers moved west in the 19th century, the area along Ashland Creek was inhabited by the Shasta Indians. Gold finds in nearby Jacksonville brought prospectors to the region. However, after gold failed to be found in any bulk, prospectors became ranchers and farmers, taking up leases and working the land. Agriculture remains an important part of the local economy.

In addition to theatre and artistic culture, Ashland offers terrific entry to the Oregon outdoors. Lithia Park runs from the centre of town up through Ashland Canyon, taking walkers through miles of hiking trails, up a fairly steep hillside that is heavily wooded in places. For very keen hikers, Ashland is only ten miles from the Pacific Crest Trail. This heavy duty hiking route runs from Mexico to Canada along the crest of mountains in California, Oregon and Washington. In other outdoor pursuits, rafting companies in the small town also offer rafting trips on the Rogue River, the nearest point is about twenty miles away, but the companies transport you there and kit you out fully for the ride. The Rogue River has some pretty dramatic rapids, a result, a walk through these neighbourhoods is like a trip to the countries themselves. As a result, the ethnic diversity means that the city has a rich mix in dining. Everything from Mongolian to Zaire to Anatolian is available – and all at good quality.

Toronto is the most populous city in Canada and the capital of Ontario. It was originally settled by the Iroquois and Huron Indians, later by the French, and then became an English trading post in the late 19th century.

Toronto is a city of high rise architecture, vast parks and, believe it or not, beaches along Lake Ontario. There are eleven beaches in total, including one that is 'clothing optional'. Given Toronto's polarised climate, the beaches don't open until June and they close in late August.

Getting around Toronto for the lone visitor is not too difficult – streetcars, a subway system and an above ground rail serve the city well. Maps are everywhere and English is the main language. Plus the downtown area, which includes shopping, dining and many of its eclectic neighbourhoods can be covered on foot. In addition, the largest airport, the one used by international flights, is served by an express train which brings passengers to downtown Toronto every 15 minutes.

The main sites to see downtown, include the freestanding CN Tower – a 500 metre high tower with a glass elevator, a glass floor at the top and a revolving restaurant.

challenge to many an expert. However, the river also has its peaceful spots, with gentle flows through dramatic redwood forests.

Ashland is an ideal place for the solo traveller because the tolerant atmosphere means that everyone who is equally tolerant is accepted. People are curious and happy to tell you about their lives and family while also taking time to hear about yours.

The nearest airport is at Medford, an industrial town about 20 miles away. You can take a taxi to Ashland, but if you plan to explore the area, then I recommend you rent a car. Orientation in the area is not difficult. The I-5 freeway acts as a link between California to the south and Washington State to the north. Ashland only has two exits from the freeway – north and south. The town is fairly linear within the valley, so getting around is easy if you orient yourself well.

Downside: Flights to Medford come from Seattle, Washington; Portland, Oregon; or San Francisco, California so there are few direct routes to the small town.

To read: *The Shack* by Wm. Paul Young was a cult classic a few years ago. It tells of a man who loses his daughter in a brutal abduction. A few years later, he receives a letter, apparently from God, inviting him to a shack in the Oregon wilderness. On the brighter note, *Sometimes a Great Notion*, by Ken Kesey (author of *One Flew Over the Cuckoo's Nest*) tells of a small Oregon town and how a strike at the local lumber mill splits a family.

Washington, DC

This city was born of politics and lives for politics. From the origins of the United States, when George Washington became its first president, much united the new nation. But it was also much divided over where the capital city should be. George Washington ultimately made the decision after the states of Maryland and Virginia donated the land. George Washington himself called it Federal City, but it was eventually named after this first president.

It was designed to have large boulevards, green public spaces so that it would feel grand, like the very best of the European capitals. And the city does feel grand. From the National Mall to Capitol Hill and out to Georgetown, there is a strong sense of space and grace.

However it is not just the seat of the US government, Washington DC is home to the United States treasures – from museums to monuments to memorials. There is so much to see, much of it all within walking distance – The White House, The Smithsonian and The Lincoln Memorial (so many, I'm keeping to only three).

This is an American city that is comfortable with visitors, is easy on the feet and that has good restaurants and a café culture.

Downside: Public transport from the international airport to the downtown area is not the easiest. The Silverline Express Bus travels from the airport and drops passengers off at a garage near the Wiehle-Reston East Metroline Station. From here, you cross a pedestrian bridge to reach the Metroline.

To read: Tom Clancy, James Patterson, Ken Follett, David Baldacci, John Gresham and other popular thriller writers all set novels in this centre of American politics.

Toronto

Toronto is one of the most ethnically and culturally diverse cities in the world. Of its 8.5 million people, more than half were born overseas. Foreign born citizens are considered to be as Canadian as those born in this vast land. This means that natives have no premium when it comes to belonging, and cultural and ethnic groups find it easier to take pride in their new nationality.

But ethnicity is not lost. While assimilation is high, newcomers contribute all their origins had to offer. Therefore Toronto has a China Town, Little India, Little Portugal, Little Italy – and more. As a

A less iconic site, but an interesting one nonetheless, is Black Creek Pioneer Village, a recreation of 19th century life in what was an outpost. On the opposing side of the social scale, you can visit Casa Loma, former home of an English financier which shows the wealth this land generated for the fortunate and hard-working few.

Among museums, the Royal Ontario Museum is an amazing crystal-like structure that contains artefacts from Ontario, Canada and the rest of the world. A more diverse museum is the Bata Shoe Museum, obviously devoted to footwear and which even contains a pair of Napoleon's socks.

Niagara Falls is around a 1.5 hours away and there are day trips from the city centre.

Toronto is worth visiting because it isn't a generic North American town, it has built itself on immigrant roots, welcoming and absorbing all newcomers and creating a peaceful and diverse community. As a result, it is to be enjoyed and appreciated for what might seem like a quiet achievement but, in this world, is quite momentous.

Downside: The winter climate can be harsh with frequent temperatures that sit below -10°C.

To read: Many of Margaret Atwood's novels are set in Toronto, particularly *Alias Grace* and *Cat's Eye*. In addition, John Irving's *A Prayer for Owen Meany* is set in this city and Yann Martel's *Life of Pi* ends here.

Taos, New Mexico

New Mexico is very different from its neighbours, mainly because it is heavily influenced by Native American and Mexican cultures. The area was colonised by the Spanish, then Mexico, and has a large Native American community. The state as a whole has adopted all three cultures giving the area a totally different feel from neighbouring Arizona or Texas.

Sante Fe is the state capital and has only 70,000 people. The largest city in New Mexico is Albuquerque, and this is the entry point for most visitors who fly in. Few international flights reach Albuquerque directly, therefore you will likely have to connect through Dallas, Phoenix, or other major cities to get here.

Taos is one of the most interesting small towns within the United States. It is famous for its artistic community, many of whom come from the local American Indian tribes. It is made up of several neighbourhoods. Taos Skiing is self-explanatory. The ski area here is challenging, novices beware. Taos Box sits alongside the Rio Grande and is well known as a river rafting area and for its outstanding scenery. Taos Pueblo is home to a Native American community and is a UNESCO World Heritage site, while Ranchos de Taos is a separate village to the south.

New Mexican buildings are quite unique, flat-roofed and square with smooth walls and squared windows.

Taos itself is small and walkable. A trolley bus tour will take those who prefer a guided tour. Much of Taos culture stems around art. The sculpture clay in the area is unique as it contains tiny fleck of mica that provide a sparkle. The painted art tends to have Native American or Mexican influence, so you should expect to buy something unique. Art galleries abound and much is expensive. However, what is free is the opportunity to sit on the square in Taos and watch the world go by as locals – Native American, Hispanic and White go about their business. The food tends to be Mexican in origin and well worth trying. The joy of this town for the traveller, especially the stranger who travels alone, is that you can blend in – no one will ask you your business, but they will exchange the time of day.

One of the things Taos is famous for that you won't see but you might hear is its 'hum'. Many people say they can hear a low continuous rumbling sound that has nothing to do with traffic or power lines. Explanations are that it is simply city people unused to a quieter locale, or it is static charge from power lines that run through the Rio Grande. Some even attribute it to UFO activity at a local secret government facility. Early in the morning or late at night is the best time to hear the 'hum'.

Downside: It isn't an easy place to reach but is probably a good place to go if you are travelling to two or three US cities. Crime is low here but drink driving is a problem. Take care on the roads.

To read: Many novels by Tony Hillerman, especially his Navajo Mysteries, are set here. In addition *The Milagro Beanfield War* by John Nicols and taking a step back in time, *The Plumed Serpent* by D.H. Lawrence.

Far East

Hong Kong

This is the perfect city for the solo traveller who has never been to the Far East but wants to visit the area and still have the security of the English language.

This was a British colony until 1996, and it blends perfectly between Chinese and British cultures – from the temples to churches and shops and markets. It's made up of a collection of islands and the southern tip of a peninsula that adjoins the Chinese mainland. Hong Kong Island, with its Victoria Peak can feel British, but travel across the ferry to Kowloon, Mong Kok and the mainland and it is easy to feel like a foreigner in a foreign land.

When it comes to getting around, thankfully the MTR metro has terrific underground transport from the airport to the mainland and to Hong Kong Island. While an above ground train can carry you out towards China.

The markets in Kowloon and Mong Kok tend to be small but specialised. For instance The Bird Market sells birds, but also bird enthusiasts take their own caged birds there and let them sing among others of their own kind. The flower market sells, guess what? And the jade market, well, I hope you have guessed or you shouldn't be going anywhere alone. In Kowloon, you are likely to be hassled by street hawkers, but don't let them bother you. Simply walk on.

Everyone who visits Hong Kong Island takes the tram to The Peak – it's worth it for the view of Hong Kong Harbour. If you're visiting the island on a Sunday, you will notice young women picnicking with friends on any green space available. This is the day off for most household maids, and they throng together with friends from their home towns. Sunday is especially vibrant at Victoria Park, which is full of colourful groups of women, talking, laughing, singing and dancing. Another local site on the island is the Mid-Levels Escalator, literally an escalator that climbs the steep hillside of residences and shops. The escalator runs downhill in the morning and uphill in the afternoon – all to chime with the travels of school children, housewives and commuters.

For the best journey between the island and Kowloon take the ferry – it feels old and exotic, especially when dhows in full sail pass by.

The solo traveller can get lost, gloriously so, in Hong Kong.

Downside: Some people might find it a little intense. My advice is simply to remember to sit in a café, watch people and breathe.

To read: Paul Theroux and his *Kowloon Tong: A Novel of Hong Kong* which focuses on the time when colonial rule in the city ended. If you like short stories, then try *Love in a Forbidden City* by Eileen Chang.

Ubud, Indonesia

Firstly, forget the book *Eat, Pray, Love*. Ubud is a wonderful place to visit and an easy foray into solo travel in the Far East. This small town is located in the interior of the island of Bali, surrounded by lush rice paddies and overgrown foliage. It is also the cultural centre of Bali with theatre, music and art all valued, practised and often on display.

Ubud's history goes back to the 8th century when a Hindu priest meditated at the confluence of the two local rivers. It has grown slowly, and technically isn't a town but a network of 14 villages, all run by a village committee. It has three main streets with small lanes that intersect. The Royal Palace is still occupied by descendants and most of the property is open to the public. The Monkey Forest is on the outskirts of town and full of hungry monkeys. Take no food, not even any that is wrapped and sealed – these primates have good noses and are aggressive thieves. Temples, art galleries, open air theatre abound in Ubud. Tours from the town will also take you to the Elephant Cave, hot springs and the volcano.

Ubud bustles and it is easy for the solo traveller to merge into its flow. Art classes plus yoga, cookery and a variety of therapies are all on offer. There are traditional markets at night and during the day. And, if you feel like some alone time, the paths out of town offer relaxing walks through rice paddies and lush vegetation.

There are buses from the main tourist beaches of Bali to Ubud. At the airport there is a clearly designated taxi stand, use this to take a cab and fares to specific destinations are prescribed but confirm this with the driver before you take off.

Downside: Ubud has grown in a haphazard fashion over the last twelve centuries. Its small streets and lanes are not ready for the hefty traffic that sometimes appears here.

To read: *Balilicious* by Becky Wicks as is the antidote to *Eat, Pray, Love*. While Liz Gilbert found bliss, Wicks finds wry humour. *Bali Conspiracy Most Foul: Inspector Singh Investigates* by Shamini Flint is a murder mystery but with a Balinese kick.

Delhi, India

Now Delhi might sound like a strange place to recommend to the solo traveller, but its buzz and vibrancy make it an easy city to absorb the solo traveller and help you to blend in.

However, the first thing I have to recommend is a good hotel – read the reviews carefully. Often in India it is true that the more expensive the hotel then the less likely you are to encounter Delhi-belly and all that ensues. So try and book as expensive as you can afford – use the review sites to shop for the cheapest room rates.

With that over, I should tell you why to visit Delhi. First, it's the people. They talk to you – there is no anonymity here. They will remember you. Then it's the colours. Women wear such an array of vibrant hues that your eyes are kept busy taking it all in.

Shopping in Delhi is a wonderful experience. You don't have to shop much or spend a lot of money, simply enjoy the experience and remember to haggle. There are charlatan shopkeepers. Connaught Place, at the centre of Delhi (now called Rajiv Chawk, although no one uses that name) is two concentric rings and crammed with shops. The traders will tell you that their goods truly come from Rajasthan, Kerala or Punjab, but you can never be sure. Try and find the Cottage Emporium, just off one of the streets stretching out of Connaught

Place. It is government run with stalls from every part of India, therefore a Kashmiri pashmina bought here should truly be from Kashmir (this might not be the case in other shops). Remember to haggle. You don't have to be rude, simply offer one third less than they ask, be prepared to come up a little in price, also be prepared to walk if you don't feel it is a fair price.

A more modern chain of shops worth visiting is Fab India – all indoor, all air-conditioned and none allow haggling. This is a terrific place to buy silk blouses, dresses, curtains (they deck my sitting room) and most manner of housewares.

Also visit a book shop. Traders sell the latest western best sellers at roadsides, but it is worth visiting an Indian book shop. They look like they are stocked haphazardly with no apparent order on the shelves, but ask for any title and it is likely that the bookseller knows exactly where it is.

When it comes to things to see in Delhi, well you do need to sit with your guide book and plan. I heartily recommend Humayun's Tomb. It was built before the Taj Mahal (work began in 1562) and commissioned by a wife grieving for her husband. However, it is red sandstone rather than white marble, and impressive nonetheless. There is also the Mughal Red Fort, 17th century, and the 12th century Qutub complex.

When it comes to getting around, talk to a taxi driver outside your hotel grounds (within the grounds makes it more expensive). Tell the driver where you want to go, list multiple destinations and know whether you want to be out for the day or the half day. The driver will give you a price and be your personal driver for the day.

There is so much to see and experience here that it truly is essential to bring a good guide book. It will be your bible, simply don't take it out in the street.

Downside: Delhi can be overwhelming, be prepared to step back to your hotel for a few hours. Don't do too much in one day.

To read: The best known novel set in Delhi outside of India is *White Tiger* by Aravind Adiga, a dark tale of greed and revenge. Ruskin Bond and his *The Room on the Roof,* which is Bond's semi-autobiographical tale of growing up in post-colonial India.

And now a word from our editor on how not to do it

Many friends find it strange that I would ever travel alone. After all, I have a husband; why not go along with him? Couples go on adventures all the time, especially after their children have left home. Well, sometimes I do travel with my husband, but for so many reasons, travelling alone has an appeal. The freedom to watch people without interruption, the opportunity to decide where to go, how to spend my time, when to walk, when to eat – need I go on? Plus my husband likes to travel painlessly, without hiccups – as though all the elements are cogs in a watch. I prefer some hitches (certainly not many and nothing major) and love the sense of overcoming those difficulties. Paul Theroux, a travel writer who loves to go solo, once said that travel was great inconvenience interrupted by the occasional epiphany. I certainly believe that – we need the difficult times to make the joys in our journey truly shine.

I was only nineteen when I saw an ad in the back of a student newspaper offering trips overland to Greece for £49. I was a poor student, as were all my friends. I remember showing them the advertisement that to me screamed adventure.

They all, each one, shook their heads and said simply that they couldn't afford to go. What was I to do? Ignore the yearning, bend over my books and pretend I had never seen this opportunity, this lure? A classics teacher had told me tales of Orpheus, Theseus and Odysseus, and the idea that I could visit their land of adventure entranced me. So I saved from my meagre grant. Interestingly, I can't remember what I deprived myself of so it couldn't have been very important.

Until that moment, I'd never been overseas. Family and friends tried to tell me it was a crazy idea to go it alone, dangerous – and they were right. I didn't sleep on the overnight bus journey to London, and my tiredness grew while wandering around London lugging a hefty suitcase (no wheels in those days) while waiting for the coach to take me to my promised land. When I finally shut my eyes on the open deck of the ferry between Dover and Oostende I had no idea that I would waken to five male faces staring at me as I drooled in slumber. Thankfully, truly thankfully, there were three female students on the coach to Greece and they let me tag along as their fourth. This was a huge help when we were pitched out of the bus in a Greek city and told a representative from the travel company would meet us. We stood on a street corner for hours, smiling at every stranger, hoping they might, just might, be the travel representative we waited for. But no one stopped, no one collected us. After three hours in a hot city street, that was growing less exotic as beggars and leering men edged closer, a passing Tourist Police Officer came to our aid. He took us to his office, gave us water and sweet buns, made some phone calls and put us in a (free) taxi to our destination.

I was fortunate that I found three girls so willing to take in a fourth. Heavens knows what would have happened if I had been left on the Greek street alone. But my planning didn't improve. My next solo trip was to Portugal – again my friends had no desire to join me when I told them I'd found a cheap flight. It was a package trip flight and I was the only passenger not wrapped up in a flight-hotel deal. I took pleasure in knowing that I was the only independent traveller on board. That was until we landed. It was late when the aircraft touched down, the airport bank was shut, and there was nowhere to change pounds to escudos (no holes in the walls in those days). I watched the package tourists line up for their coaches and a group of local boys watched me as I silently fretted over how I was going to get to town with no local money. I asked around the travel representatives to find out if any would exchange money with me. One of the reps did more than that. She gave me a seat on her coach, dropped me off at a B&B and pointed to the bank where I could change money in the morning.

The kindness of strangers has bailed me out of problems many times. From missed meetings in

Italy (no mobile phones and the friend I waited for was at a different train station wondering where I could be) to losing my backpack in Israel, to being stranded in the African bush overnight after our bus broke down – always strangers have stepped in to help. And it's why I have always been quick to come to the aid of foreign visitors to the UK when they need help – whether it is finding the right train, being lost in London or being abandoned by friends.

And I have to confess to feeling occasional fear on solo trips. Spooked doesn't even begin to describe how I felt as the lone visitor to a temple behind an Ikea on Hong Kong's mainland. I had that sense that I was being watched, even though there were no other visitors and apparently no staff in attendance. The atmosphere was made worse by the thousand life-sized Buddha statues that sat in attendance, and I suspected that at least one of them moved when I wasn't looking. This was a time when I wished I'd left word of my destination at the hotel's reception. However, all turned out well – it was a lonely place, a little creepy, but no one kidnapped me and I lived to tell my tale.

However, my travels have grown less organised, I'm not sure why, perhaps I've grown too confident.

Hence my last trip, when really I shouldn't have been allowed to leave home. It was a combined trip that would involve some work - editing manuscripts – and play – being joined by my husband, sister and friends. Sounds perfect. But on the flight I realised that, yet again, I'd forgotten to print out the details of where I was staying – all I could remember was one island, two locations. I appeased myself with a vague recollection and believed it would all eventually come to me. It didn't! And to make matters worse, I reached Piraeus and found a general strike – no ferries! I'd heard about the strike, but in my Pollyanna world, thought it would be over by the time I arrived. Athens is a lovely city, but I didn't want to stay there. I wanted to reach my island. Thankfully a taxi driver asked me if I were going to *X*. 'Hoping to!' I said. He pointed across the square, "Two ladies over there also want to go. I can take all three of you down the Peloponnese to catch a private ferry - $200." Between three, I knew this was as good a deal as I was going to get. My hotel on the island had a zero cancellation policy on arrival day. Added to this the cost of an Athenian hotel until the strike was over – there was no competition on cost. The taxi driver hailed the women, but they ignored him.

"Should I go and talk to them?" I asked

"Go ahead."

One sat with her laptop out on a pavement step. The other, a taller woman, looked around as if hoping for a call from heaven.

I told them I was also heading to *X* and said the taxi driver's offer was a good one.

"But what if our hotel has given out our rooms to someone else?" The tall one said.

"It's May," I told them. "Early season, the hotels will not be full."

The short one tapped away at her laptop, looking vulnerable – one fast thief and her laptop would be gone.

"Where are you from?" I asked by way of conversation. I didn't want to have to pay for the taxi fare alone, three people made it economical. The two women looked at each other as though unwilling to give away even their nationality.

"Canada," the tall one said finally.

I introduced myself – even gave my name. "Strikes happen all the time here. I come each year and have learned to be flexible, you can't always do everything you planned."

The laptop girl nodded towards the taxi driver. "But what is in it for him."

The taxi driver was an older Greek, the type I felt familiar with, pragmatic and with the English skills to help us tourists out when we don't quite understand how the country works. I've met many such Greek men through the decades. "He's making some money to pay his bills, he's helping us out at the same time." I wondered how much more I could tell her.

The tall one finally made a decision. "I would like to call the hotel and check they still have our rooms," she said and set out across the road.

CR6/17

"But where is she going?" I asked.

The short one was putting away her laptop. "To find a call box," she said, as though it was obvious.

The taxi driver, who had joined us, called out to her. "Use my phone."

She called and told the hotel owner that she was at the port. The hotelier thought it was the port across from the island and said the taxi driver was robbing us by charging 200 euros.

"You should have said you were at Pireaus," I said.

"I did!"

"No," I was growing cross. "You said 'port'."

The taxi driver had had enough. He called their hotel back on his phone. Greek can sound like an angry language, and I could see the girls grow concerned. He passed his cheap mobile back to the tall girl. A short word from the hotel owner and she nodded. I was heading to my favourite island.

My husband would have hated such disruption to his travel schedule. He's a good traveller, a frequent traveller, tells people he lives in seat 29b. But he wouldn't have seen the adventure in being in a taxi with three strangers, heading to a town you had a vague geographical sense of and answering the taxi driver's phone because the road needed two hands on the steering wheel.

We made it to the island, but I turned up at the wrong accommodation – the second hotel

91

where I wouldn't check in for another two weeks. As I sat down for a coffee and worked my way through old emails trying to find a reservation, my phone rang. It was the reservation agency to tell me about the ferry strike and that I wouldn't be able to make it to the island.

"But I'm here," I told him.

He laughed, "How?"

I gave him a quick outline of the journey and was able to ask him a very important question. "Which hotel am I booked into?"

He laughed again. And told me where I would find my room and my bed.

All very fortunate, all part of the adventure.

Lightning Source UK Ltd.
Milton Keynes UK
UKOW05f0014051216
289181UK00008B/32/P